GW0047020202

THE THIRD TOWER

JOURNEYS IN ITALY

ANTAL SZERB

THE THIRD TOWER

JOURNEYS IN ITALY

Translated from the Hungarian by
Len Rix

PUSHKIN PRESS
LONDON

Pushkin Press
71–75 Shelton Street, London WC2H 9JQ

The Third Tower was first published in Hungarian as
A harmadik torony; Budapest, 1936

This translation first published by Pushkin Press in 2014

ISBN 978 1 782270 53 9

Frontispiece: *Antal Szerb*
© Petőfi Literary Museum, Budapest

Image credits on page 107

Set in 10 on 13 Monotype Baskerville
by Tetragon, London

Proudly printed and bound in Great Britain
by TJ International, Padstow, Cornwall
on Munken Premium White 90gsm

www.pushkinpress.com

CONTENTS

TRANSLATOR'S
INTRODUCTION

A UGUST 1936. The early-morning train is pulling into Venice, on time to the minute and crammed with happy, chattering people. Among them are the usual foreigners, mostly German, but today, as throughout this remarkable summer, they are overwhelmingly Italian, people of all ages and social classes, taking advantage of the cheap fares now available on the *treni popolari*. For this is Mussolini's Italy, things are on the rise, and the whole country is caught up in the restless, happy excitement of a new era, bonded in common purpose at home, delirious with military success abroad. Abyssinia has been conquered; in Spain, Italian troops are triumphantly on the march; from Greece, Turkey and Africa, reporters pen ecstatic reminders of the extent of former Italian power. It is a country where, if you believe the papers, "only wonderful things" seem to happen.

The train has now come to a halt and stands steaming in the steadily rising heat. Among the disembarking throng, with their battered suitcases and endless excited chatter, is a diminutive, nervously smiling man in a large black hat. Sallow-skinned, he too could be Italian, possibly Jewish. He, too, should be moving along with the crowd, for he has yet to find somewhere to stay: his decision to come was made at the last minute, on a panic impulse, with no time to arrange anything. But to travel is one thing, to arrive another. He seems momentarily lost. Perhaps it is dawning on him, rather belatedly, that his reasons for coming had not been all they had seemed. For him Italy, Venice in particular, had never been a place of mere "travel". It had meant too much to him, for far too long; had possessed him, at times, like a narcotic. It lay at the epicentre of a long-standing spiritual crisis, begun in adolescence, unduly protracted, perhaps not quite over yet.

It should be over. He is now thirty-five years of age, an assimilated Hungarian of Jewish descent, and has done much to establish himself both as a man and in the eyes of his fellow countrymen. His star (not yet a yellow one) is in the ascendant. His scholarly works (various monographs, a groundbreaking *History of Hungarian Literature*) have won him serious academic recognition, to which his first novel, *The Pendragon Legend* (set in England and Wales), has added a wide popularity; his finest work is still to come. But there are limits. He still teaches, on a modest salary, not in the university where he rightly belongs, but in a commercial secondary school, for which he is by temperament totally unsuited, and where his pupils adore him. For, despite his formidable erudition and rising reputation, he is the gentlest, kindest, most self-effacing of men.

But time is not on his side, in any sense of the term: not this morning, if he is to find somewhere to rest his head; not for all the things he so desperately wants to see and re-experience on this visit. In truth, not ever. Whenever he comes to Venice, he now remembers, he sees it with the intensity of a dying man setting eyes on it for the last time. This time, he already half knows, it will be.

A thirty-five-year-old Hungarian arriving on the train to Venice… Readers of *Journey by Moonlight* will sense what is coming next. In Venice, despite the teeming crowds and the oppressive heat, he is filled with an intense elation that rises, in the dark little back alleys, to an unspeakable "ecstasy". There he experiences once again the old, overwhelming "nostalgia"—too simple a word for the death-haunted, spiritual-erotic states of consciousness that had blighted his youth. Like Mihály, the hero of the novel (begun soon after his return home), he might reasonably have thought that having at last become a "serious person" he would now be safe from the "danger that Italy represented". In the novel, with casual, indifferent ease, Venice lays that fantasy to rest. The hero's painfully forged adult persona is stripped away, and his journey becomes an increasingly headlong descent into mental breakdown and spiritual despair.

The novel, undoubtedly, was written to exorcize those ghosts for ever, to purge its author once and for all of the follies, the "madness" of his youth. What raises it to the level of a masterpiece is not so much the subtlety of its language, or the elegant symmetry of its construction, but the unsparing intelligence, the relentless self-irony and the moments of wry humour that give it authority. None of that authority would have been possible without this difficult visit, made in 1936, at what should have been the midpoint of his life, amid war and rumours of war.

Mihály's journey, though downwards and by "moon-light", is ever towards self-knowledge, though ending in defeat. But his author, even as he savours the old heady poison of nostalgia, finds that it need no longer be his master. As his narrative proceeds, the tone, always engagingly personal with this writer, grows increasingly relaxed and playful. But he leaves us with a last, sideways glimpse of the power Venice once held over him. Of the ubiquitous mask he writes, in farewell to the city: "In Casanova's day the mask *was* Venice. The hideous, beaklike visor held some essence, something demonic, some ancient principle of evil, that was so old and so refined that even today it stirs us no less powerfully than goodness and great acts of love."

The route he follows, in successive packed and chattering *treni popolari* down to Ravenna, remains many-layered, recapitulating the steps both of his own earlier self (or selves) and of the mythical heroes of his youth.

During his first stop, Palladio's Vicenza, the broad question of Italy and what it stands for in the "Northern mind" is brought into focus. His thoughts turn naturally to his admired Goethe, who first "discovered" the great neo-classical architect, and who inspired Szerb with his vision of the interconnectedness of all European culture—the theme of his great literary histories. But here we see another effect of layering: when he talks of Palladio's art working, in combination with the mystical "serenity" of Italy itself, to "quell the Furies in Goethe's soul, cleansing and purifying it", does he allude to a process he feels beginning now in himself? If so, its precise workings, and quite where they might lead, remain unclear.

In Verona, despite its association with another of his mythical heroes, Szerb is forced to retreat. The pressure of modern Italy, and his increasingly uncertain place in it, suddenly become "too much", and he flees to Lake Garda. The inner journey likewise takes a change of direction. Up in the hills he begins to muse on self and solitude—the preoccupation that will dominate the rest of the journey.

In this wandering and oblique passage towards ever-greater self-knowledge, his beloved Italy plays no small role. Chiefly, it forces a relentless series of disillusion-ments, sometimes gentle, more often brutal, upon him. There is something touchingly comic in the thought of our mild-mannered, hypersensitive, introverted little author, locked in his musings on history and the "Northern soul", being cheerfully jostled on crowded trains, slapped on the back (for our Hungarian friends are currently all the fashion), and tormented by the happy revellers who fill his "historic" little room above the famously picturesque square in Verona (specially recommended by Baedeker) with guffawing, singing and shouting long into the night. But there is a darker side to all this jollity. Events offstage—in Spain, Abyssinia and elsewhere—are never far from his mind. His journey continues, taking in new sights, revisiting "monuments from his private past", but the eyes that view them become increasingly dispassionate.

Most venerated of all are the last items on the itinerary: the sacred mosaics of the San Vitale, in Ravenna. More than anything, they had represented the tortured spiritual yearnings of his adolescence—as so memorably evoked in *Journey by Moonlight*:

> Elbows on the table, they studied the plates, whose gold backgrounds glittered up at them like a mysterious fountain of light at the bottom of a mineshaft. Within the Byzantine pictures there was something that stirred a sleeping horror in the depth of their souls. At a quarter to twelve they put on their overcoats, and, with ice in their hearts, set off for midnight mass…
> For a month afterwards it was all Ravenna, and for Mihály Ravenna had remained to that day an indefinable species of dread.

Like the sinister back alleys of Venice, they are another critical test for him. There is a world of buried anguish, but also of relief, as it slowly dawns on him: "So, this was the real goal of my travels, this run-down and evil-smelling town."

It is almost the end of the road. His journey is effectively over, its purpose seemingly accomplished. The way home lies through Trieste, another historic city with a wealth of associations, should he still be in the mood.

But all Szerb's writing contains an element of surprise, and though he doesn't know it yet, the most important discovery is still to come. Italy has retained its greatest gift for him for the last. It is one that will sustain him in the difficult times ahead, just a short way down the road, when rumours of war are no longer just rumours, and all question of travel has, for him, finally come to an end.

LEN RIX, 2013

THE THIRD
TOWER

I INITIALLY wanted to go to Spain, but Spain, in this most horrific summer in all its history, did not seem a very welcoming place, with its opposing radio stations taking turns to howl in triumph over the destruction of everything in the world for which one would want to visit that country. Perhaps I shall never get there now; and if I did, I would no longer find what I went to see. From time to time history seems to forget a particular city or citadel—a Nuremberg, an Oxford, a Toledo— tucked away behind its back. But this is mere absent-mindedness: a signal arrives, and amid wars, revolutions, catastrophic upheaval and the hammer blows of "progress", its impermanence is laid bare.

Then it occurred to me that I simply must go to Italy—while Italy remains where it is, and while going there is still possible. Who knows for how much longer that will be; indeed, for how much longer I, or any of us, will be able to go anywhere? The way events are moving, no one will be allowed to set foot outside his own country. The Germans have long found it almost impossible to venture abroad, with a fine of a thousand marks for attempting to visit Austria. The Russians too have been denied this right for a great many years. Foreign travel is not one of life's basic needs. No doubt the totalitarian state will sooner or later decree that the true patriot is the one who stays at home.

And this is why, whenever I travel to Italy, I go there as if for the very last time, and why, when I first set eyes on any of its towns, it is as if I am not just returning, but bidding it farewell. Dostoevsky writes that we should live as if our every minute were the last moments of a man condemned to death: that way, we would grasp the ineffable richness of life. My impressions of Italy always feel like the last visions of a dying man.

TO BE IN VENICE

I TRAVELLED to Italy in a headlong rush, a blind panic, only half packed, without attending upon the deities of the National Bank's foreign exchange department, barely pausing for breath, straight to Venice. The heat was sweltering, the city bursting at the seams, and I was moved on, with varying degrees of brusqueness, from hotel to hotel. They say the city had never known such a season. The Spanish resorts were being bombed, and in the French ones the waiters were going on strike at every second mealtime. In the early morning, when the late-to-bed had finally retired and before the early risers were up, there was not a single lodging, of any description, to be had in the city—if we ignore the odd German dozing until dawn on the coffee-house terraces to save the expense of a hotel. It was certainly not pleasant to arrive in the heat, in this pampered city, crammed as it was with the world's fashionable riffraff, and be forced to wander for hours looking for somewhere to lay my head. But I drew enormous comfort from the simple fact that *I was there*. Whether things were going well or badly, whether I was miserable or happy, meant nothing beside the fact that it was *there*, in Venice, that I was happy or unhappy, that things were going well or badly. Life is not always and everywhere uniformly "real". How wise were the great scholastics who distinguished between degrees of being, rising by regular gradations of reality towards perfection.

No, I didn't "enjoy myself" or "feel at home" in Venice, in the commonly accepted, physical-emotional sense of these terms. But, for the entire length of my stay, I was filled with elation by the mere fact that I was there, and that, by sharing in the life of that exalted sphere, I was more completely myself.

IN PRAISE OF VENICE

V ENICE IS the centre of the world. Or rather, one
of its centres, for the world has several. It tilts on
various axes, its prevailing truths are legion; the "one
thing needful" takes many different forms. In St Mark's
Square you really have a sense of being at the centre of
the world—just as you do in several places in Rome, or
at the Place de l'Opéra in Paris. London has none of
these sites. London may be the greatest city on Earth,
and the most populous, but it remains somewhere out
on the periphery, not at the centre. It has no St Mark's
Square. Following Valery Larbaud's principle, one might
describe it as village-like in its isolation. A man strolling
around St Mark's Square knows that by doing so he is
performing a kind of function, just being there, at the
centre of the world, letting the world revolve around
him.

Venice is the city of intimate closeness. The most
human-scale of all cities. Here Western culture's Faustian
rush to infinite expansion comes to a halt. Venice cannot
"develop". It cannot become any larger than it already

is, because every square inch of available dry land has long been crammed full. Nor is there very much of it. Wherever you set out from, the city can be traversed from one end to the other in half an hour, almost all of it on foot. Everything is to hand, and distant objects are brought close enough to touch. Great seafaring ships make their way between the rows of houses, for here the wide ocean comes home. That is perhaps why Venice is more of a city than any other. It holds more. It is more of a home.

Darkness is gathering over the lagoon where it touches St Mark's Square, bringing the silhouette of San Giorgio Maggiore, the Giudecca Island and Santa Maria della Salute into sharp relief, and making them more than ever the standard schoolroom example—a paradigm of inflection, like *amo-amas-amat*—of the beauty of land-scape and the works of man. And the soft radiance of its brick-pink serenity spills out over the city—this city that exists in the spontaneous sense of nostalgia experienced by everyone who feels, on arrival, that he must have been here before, though he has never previously set eyes on it.

THE BACK ALLEYS

AND ONCE AGAIN, with the same expectation and excitement, I wander through the back alleys of Venice. These streets are wonderfully narrow. There are some so narrow that two overweight men cannot pass through them walking side by side. Even the broader ones are only wide enough for the traffic of a bygone age. One Easter Sunday I saw for myself how one of these passageways can become so crowded that the flow comes to a complete stop, unable to move forward or go back. Only very slowly, step by step, after a good half-hour's wriggling and squeezing, could you fight your way free from a street just one hundred metres long.

If I were compelled to speak with total candour, I would say that it is for these back alleys that I love Italy. For me, they represent what gardens were to the age of Goethe, and what "Nature" was to the Romantics. No snow-covered peak, no glacier, mountain lake or stream, no sea or parkland could ever move me like the back alleys of an old Italian city. My dreams, my moods of nostalgia, lead me thither. The first time I set eyes on an

Italian hilltop town with these same tiny streets I felt the deepest ecstasy I had ever known.

What this is in me I do not know. Under the influence of these little passageways I experience an altered state so deep I simply cannot regard it as the sort of emotion you would expect from a historically minded person; it is so much more intense and instinctive. I am aware of the usual Freudian explanation, and it bores me. It is so plausible I no longer believe it.

PENSIONE

I N THE FIRST HOTEL that promised an available room, the waiter spoke French. I panicked. Instinct told me, as the event confirmed, that the French language would not come cheap there. Where they address you in German, it is because they know you have no money; where the language is French, they take you for a member of the aristocracy. I did not linger in that particular establishment. Eventually I came to anchor in a little *pensione* that nestled, in the most historical way imaginable (embedded, as it were, in world history), in a building right beside the Clock Tower, the Torre dell'Orologio, in St Mark's Square, by the entrance to the Merceria. From my window I can study some of the more intimate details of the Basilica. Directly above my head the two bronze men bong out the hours. I feel as a mouse would in a slipper of the great Doge Morosini.

The food here is tolerable. The tiny window of the dining room opens onto St Mark's Square. The guests speak various dialects of French and German. A French family: two mothers (or, rather, one of them must be a mother, though I can't work out which) and two daughters. You would think that gaucherie was the preserve of the Northern races, but from my observation of these two French ladies and other French guests they offer strong competition to the Germans. It's just that theirs is a different sort of gaucherie: more gracious. Or is this just my prejudice?

UNGHERIA

THE ITALIANS adore Hungary. Every day you read in the papers: "Family house on Lake Balaton", or "Nostalgie di Halászbástya". (For them, as I see it, "nostalgia" signifies "ambience" or "atmosphere"—what a wise language!) And people respond most warmly when they hear the word "Ungheria". I get the impression that the name implies almost as much for Italians as "Italy" does for us—a friendly, romantic and fundamentally different country. What attracts us to them is that everything there is so old, and what attracts them to us is that everything we have is so new—a closely related thing. I once watched a group of Italian tourists gazing in reverence at the Pasaréti Church: they had never before seen such a new one.

I was once asked in England how I could possibly have left my own highly romantic country for such a grey, petty-bourgeois place. Naturally my questioners were Italian.

THE SECRET OF
ST MARK'S

THE VAST, classical Square and the Byzantine Basilica of St Mark form an organic whole, but logically speaking they are mutually contradictory. The Procuratorial buildings and the Piazza represent the culmination of European culture: the Basilica is primordial, barbarically gilded, primitive, pre-European, older than anything European. When it was built, Europe had not yet fully decided to become what it now is. It might have been another Byzantium.

Over its portal one sees an iron grill of which any village blacksmith today would be ashamed. What a rudimentary lion stands atop St Mark's column on the quay... and the Don Quixote on the column opposite! The two porphyry lions behind the Basilica are so childishly clumsy you feel compelled to stroke their manes. I see these same red lions again and again in Northern Europe, crouching tamely in front of churches, as if begging for alms.

31

hat does mere technique matter? Here, the
verything. St Mark's Square is no larger than
s Dóm Tér, but what miraculous *grandezza*, in
its immediate setting and the wider Venetian context!
Its very grandeur stems from this contradiction: that,
small as the place was, they never stinted on the offer-
ings they made to their own greatness. And the secret of
the Basilica is that when Venice was still no more than
a clearing in the jungle, in the European middle ages,
they could sacrifice so much gold, and physical labour,
and beauty, to their God and patron saint. If St Mark's
were built today, would it genuinely please as much, for
example, as the Duomo in Florence? I doubt it. The
Campanile is a modern construction, and one senses
a certain sacrilege about it. The Basilica of St Mark is
modern in no sense at all.

But... why do they always play the *Blue Danube* and
Die Fledermaus?

SAN ZANIPOLO

THIS IS WHERE the doges rest, after their labours ruling the city. In front of it, the equestrian statue of Bartolomeo Colleoni—the quintessential equestrian statue and reference point for every subsequent such tribute to kings and generals. None of them surpasses the grim, manly features of the *condottiere*, or the perfect unity of horse and rider so justly admired by art historians. But inside the Basilica I saw a tomb on which the dead man was no less inseparable from his coffin than the *condottiere* from his horse. I found that much more affecting. Not everyone comes into the world associated with a horse. But with a coffin...

The impermanence of things. Venice found itself on the road to annihilation once before, at the start of the nineteenth century, an appalling decline that was eventually arrested. But for how much longer? Here in the Zanipolo, standing above the tombs of the doges, I am filled once again by that overpowering vision that haunts all of us who concern ourselves with the inner workings of history and Schiller's "prophecy of hindsight". The time will come when the human race, horribly reduced in numbers, will scrabble for a living in the mansions of the world's great cities like troglodytes in caves. We can see this process already beginning in some of the oldest metropolitan centres: at the Place des Vosges in Paris, in the Orsini Palace in Rome, and here in Venice in the more outlying palazzi along the Grand Canal. First will come a time when the Ducal Palace is divided into tiny bedroom-and-kitchen flats; then a time when even they are no longer needed. This is how antiquity itself passed away: there were centuries during which Rome had no more inhabitants than a village. The Eskimo scene in Madách's *The Tragedy of Man* is set in the world of the natural sciences. If Madách were writing today he would surely have placed this episode not in the polar regions but in St Mark's Square, or the Place de l'Opéra in Paris, and Eve would emerge not from an igloo, but from the ruins of a stairway leading down to the Métro.

A THOUGHT

I CANNOT DECIDE which was here first, the water or the houses. I think it must have been the water; but how is it that the water should begin so precisely where the houses end? One has the impression that they must have built the streets first and then put the water in position.

EVENING IN THE PIAZZA

AFTER DINNER I sit on the terrace of a coffee house. The square is no larger than a middle-class dining room, and yet five busy streets pour into it. It is pure theatre, Italy as represented in the opera. And the population comes and goes, rushing about in a vast crowd. It is hard to believe that there could be so many Italians—especially towards evening. All coming and going. But where to? And always along the same streets, until they are two-thirds empty.

On the coffee-house radio the Italian commentator Pluhar is reporting on some Olympic contest. His delivery is calm and expressionless; it carries no trace of his usual infectious excitement. You would have thought that the Italians...

The streets are filled with large numbers of elderly men in sailor's tops and trousers; they are indeed sailors. Among the general throng one sees the occasional figure clad in white drill and pith helmet. These are police. They stroll about in their white uniforms like Englishmen among the natives.

SIGNORAS AND
SIGNORINAS

A ND SO MANY WOMEN! Venetian women go
about bareheaded, and they are all decidedly
plain. Compared to them the women of Paris are
genuinely beautiful. There are plenty of blondes to
be seen: partly because the Venetian type, as we know
from our Burckhardt, tended to blondeness even in the
Renaissance, and partly because they follow the currently fashionable Anglo-Saxon ideal of beauty and
bleach their hair. The paradox of their faces lies in the
fair Teutonic hair and the fine-chiselled Latin features.
The two somehow do not sit well together. The faces
of the men have their own paradox: along with their
prominent Romano-Jewish noses and beautiful Southern
eyes they have ears that stick out, like the Germans. You
do see younger men who are exceedingly handsome,
but the women are not in the least attractive. But no
doubt very respectable. In Venice I saw only one street
girl, and even she was walking arm in arm with her

mother. Yet I was solicited by another, who cannot have been twelve.

There is no shortage of them. But in Italy even I am respectable. In Paris and London my amorous fantasies burned with a persistent and restless flame. I imagined that within the unfamiliar houses (and the unfamiliar women, of a different racial type) lurked a whole new world of feelings and pleasures. In Italy I don't feel even the usual low level of sexual restlessness that inevitably characterizes my bachelor existence. Women simply don't interest me. In Venice I have no need of them. The reason: Venice is herself a woman, mysterious and alluring, in her brick-pink serenity.

CA' REZZONICO

THERE IS AN EXHIBITION on at the Palazzo Rezzonico: Memoirs of Eighteenth-Century Venice. I went because I was curious to see what one of these Canal Grande mansions would be like from inside, and because I am deeply drawn to the Venice of this period, Casanova's Venice. The ceiling of the main room is adorned with frescos by Tiepolo—Rococo Learning with the angel's firebrand in his fist driving out Ignorantia. Happy Eighteenth Century! Wherever did Ignorantia, thus driven out, dwell, and in what remarkable sanatorium, that she now returns in such rude health, with such renewed vigour?

So many paintings! It is interesting—and I don't fully understand why this is—that in the eighteenth century the faces that gaze out at us from portraits are generally thoughtful and fine-featured, while in the tableaux and genre paintings of the same period they are as expressionless as dolls. How different are these studies of the Rezzonico family! Centre stage is the portly, sagacious, rather cold-looking Clement XIII, Casanova's

Pope, "Papa Rezzonico" (he only ever refers to him as such, and does so frequently and with affection: he was immensely proud of him, as a Venetian). Around His Holiness stand other members of the family: a cardinal, a state councillor and the little *nipoti*, his "cousins" presumably: I've no idea what this word signifies, whether rank or function.

The pictures are dominated by masks—the masks about which I have read so much in Casanova's writings. But only now do I know how they were painted. A huge black cape, a black three-pointed hat and the white face mask attached, with a terrifying beaklike nose, the whole producing an effect of powerful mystery and menace. They could be in a detective film, were they not somehow spiritual and altogether of a higher order. The gentlemen of the city wore such masks during the Carnival so that they could mingle freely with the populace without dishonouring their rank, and, since the Carnival could last for months, that is how long they would wear them. In Casanova's day the mask *was* Venice. The hideous, beaklike visor held some essence, something demonic, some ancient principle of evil, that was so old and so refined that even today it stirs us no less powerfully than goodness and great acts of love.

VICENZA

T HIS QUIET COUNTRY TOWN is famous for Palladio, the last great architect of the Renaissance, who lived and worked here. He achieved especial renown when his art was discovered by Goethe, for it was here that Goethe first encountered the characteristic harmony of his lines, the purity of his Classicism. The Northern psyche is essentially inward-looking: at Versailles the Germans exclaimed aloud at the imperial magnificence of the place, but here in Vicenza they found what most sublimely expressed their soul.

Not the least aspect of the grandeur of Italy is that so many of the events that shaped that Northern psyche took place in this part of the world. The greatest of the Northern peoples—the legendary heroes of the *Völkerwanderung* (the "Age of Migrations") and the visionary emperors of the Middle Ages—lived and died here. They all shared a deep love of Italy. Later, in gentler and more harmonious times, the warriors were succeeded by poets, and, in more literary centuries, by a holy trinity of English lyricists. Here the great

Lord Byron, that marvellous barnstormer, lived and loved; here John Keats, the passionate celebrant of the Grecian urn, came to exhale his dying breath; and here the corpse of the angel-faced Shelley was burnt on the pyre. As we travel further south we meet their footsteps everywhere, until we find ourselves at last in Rome, standing, profoundly moved, beside the graves of two of the trio, in the little cemetery beside the tomb of Cestius that Shelley described as accurately as if he had seen it himself. Perhaps Italy would not be Italy if the dreams of these men from the North did not still hover over its landscapes, and if it were not, at least in the minds of the poets, at once the most vividly real and the most fantastical of all countries. What would I have ever known about Italy had those intellectual giants of earlier times not come here, three of them English, and three German: Goethe, seeking the line of antique purity, Jean Paul, the paradisal wanderer, and Eichendorff, for whom the summer nights of Italy held a mystical significance?

So here came Goethe, in his great cloak and enormous hat, to gaze at Palladio's noble buildings, to take an interest in the way ordinary people dressed and in what they ate, to attend a meeting of the Academy of Olympus, and to regret that the poets of his own country could not similarly present themselves in the marketplace

to display their national art (*persönlich belustigen*). And even as he stood there contemplating these thoughts, the *Iphigenia* was taking shape inside him. Palladio's harmony had quelled the Furies in his soul, had cleansed and purified it, much as Iphigenia had done for Orestes. The serenity of Italy, that ultimate vision of the calm perfection of the soul, flooded into him. That is what his name stands for in the memory of mankind.

As I stood there myself, gazing at the harmonious lines of a Palladian villa, I could see only what was Goethe-like, what spoke of his *Iphigenia*. Some miraculous pre-existing harmony seems to operate in the human soul: an architect is born in Italy and creates certain works so that two hundred years later a poet can arrive from Germany and, through those works, come to understand himself and his destiny. Meanwhile, in all that time, how many nations, and how many generations, have annihilated one another! Mihály Babits is right when he tells us: "Great minds call to one other across time and space."

VERONA

A GRIMLY HANDSOME CITY. It was through its southern portal that the Northern invaders burst into Italy. Theodoric the Great gave it its name by associating it with Dietrich von Bern, the most potent figure in the ancient myths of the conquering Northerners, the wild hunter who charges headlong in all his Goth (and Gothic) restlessness across the bronze gates of the Cathedral of St Zeno.

It was ruled by that most virile of city dynasties, the Scaligers. Their name is preserved in the city emblem of the ladder and in two splendid tombs, the Can Grande (the Great Dog) and the Can Signorino (the Princely Dog). What expressive, and what Red Indian sounding epithets! In the court of Cangrande himself Florence's most famous exile lived and pined away to his death, after years of climbing the steps to other men's houses and eating alien bread.

I arrived at a bad moment. It was Ferragosto, the 15th of August, and to cap it all there were outdoor games in the Arena for which the whole of Italy had turned up, travelling on spectacularly discounted tickets. In the city you no sooner worked your way past one Italian tourist than you bumped into another. It was like being in Salzburg—a cut-price, petty-bourgeois, Fascist Salzburg.

I panicked and took refuge in the Cathedral. There, as if it were the most natural thing in the world, some tiny children were finishing their devotions beneath Titian's *Annunciation*. Who knows what mischief they might have got into had it not been under his eye that they said their Hail Marys? I stepped outside, into the nearby Church of St Zeno, with its quite astonishing air of solitary grandeur, then made my way back to the Castelvecchio, the old fortress of the Scaligers, from which they controlled the city and surrounding countryside.

A bridge, built in the same style as the fortress, extends the city beyond the rushing waters of the Adige. By the "same style" I mean of course the familiar red brickwork and battlements in MMMMM formation that line the tops of walls and houses and represent the Italian Gothic. They are at once formidable, like the feathered headdress of a Red Indian chieftain, and a childish masquerade. You really have to see these battlements (they adorn city halls everywhere) to understand the significance of these local dynasties. All of them—here the Scaligers, in Bologna the Bentivoglios, in Ravenna the Polentas, and in Rimini the appalling Malatestas, all so supremely unforgettable that they haunt every step of my present travels—were really just city mayors fitted out with Indian headdresses. Their protégés were regarded less as town councillors than as a praetorian guard, and they overcame their opponents not with stonemasonry saws but with daggers.

It was now evening, and I was tired. I made my way back to the Piazza Bra and seated myself on the terrazzo of a coffee house. I wanted to watch the crowd strolling around the square before going on to the performance in the Arena. "Wonderful," I said to myself. "This is exactly what they were doing in Goethe's day, and even before that—everyone so friendly, the men looking so intelligent and wise… and while Italian women are not exactly beautiful, at this time of day they seem as mysterious as objects. But so many people! So many, many people."

I found I couldn't take any more, and set off in search of dinner.

THE CONFESSION
OF A BOURGEOIS

A ND THEN IT BEGAN. In fact it had already started, on that crowded train. But it was only now that I became aware of it.

The larger restaurants were crammed to bursting with the festive hordes, so I wandered about until I found a splendidly ancient cul-de-sac, or rather courtyard, leading off a wonderfully historic street, with tables laid out for dinner. A *trattoria*. I sat down beside an ancient wall, removed my coat like everyone else, and the pretty waitress brought me an excellent *pasta asciutta* and other local dishes.

And yet I didn't feel at all comfortable. A painful childhood memory had suddenly assailed me. The feelings children have about incidents in family life are much more strongly developed (at least in my own experience) than adults generally realize. And they are perhaps even more intense than those of adults, because instinctive and without boundaries. We all know that the first question the little dears ask in the playground is, "What does your father do?" and only if they get the correct answer will they start to make friends. Children are incapable of making allowances for differences of social class. (Most dogs are the same.)

And it now came back to me that when I was a child and we used to travel abroad there would be times when my father, in an uncharacteristic fit of penny-pinching, and knowing that none of his acquaintance would be likely to see him, would take us to the sort of lower-class restaurant, like the one I was sitting in now, that he would normally never set foot in. Even then, as a child, I was filled with shame. I felt both humiliated and crushed, and I deeply pitied my parents because I imagined they must be suffering even more than I was.

And now in Verona, after I had looked around the little historic courtyard and decided that my fellow diners must all be the janitors of large tenement blocks, and it had transpired, after a few brief words with the man sharing the table with me, that he was a chauffeur, I was seized by that same childhood feeling. But I am no longer a child: I am no longer free to submit to such things. In my chequered youth I had eaten with even poorer people, not out of choice but financial constraint, and certainly not in such a historic courtyard or with such good fare. But it was no use. I didn't feel at all comfortable. I paid my bill and went to the hotel.

There, things simply got worse. It was quite a good hotel, right on the Piazza Erbe, which, according to Baedeker (and he should know), is the most picturesque town square in all Italy. I took in little of this picturesque quality, for reasons that will immediately become apparent. I had not been able to find a room in all Verona: this was the only place to offer me one—adding, "You must take it as you find it."

What I found was a positively microscopic attic room, and what was especially worrying was that the door didn't sit in the frame as it should have, nor did it close properly. Furthermore, the window was nowhere near the top of the wall, but at the bottom, in the true historic manner. Had I lain on my stomach I could have looked straight down onto the picturesque Piazza Erbe. None of this had really bothered me at midday when I took the room. I told myself it would do for one night, and that in my chequered youth I had slept in far worse, and plenty of those too. But when I came back to it at night, with my middle-class sensibilities in turmoil, that room became a torture chamber.

It was appallingly hot. The authentic floor-level window let in very little air but a great many mosquitoes.

Moreover, the room, by means of the door that wouldn't close, adjoined another, one of those long corridor-like rooms you often find in Italian hotels in which they store linen and household implements and carry out ironing and other such chores. But now, in view of the flood of visitors, even that had been made available—to an elderly and completely insane Italian. Twice in the course of the night, each time just as I was drifting off to sleep, he barged into my room and, when I shouted at him, withdrew, uttering incomprehensible noises. True, I had my revenge. As soon as I reckoned he would be, as I had been, on the point of sleep, I opened my door softly, like a ghost, and then shut it again in the same soft and ghostly manner, and made eerie wailing noises.

To add to the fun, the entire festive, travel-subsidized population of Italy had chosen the occasion to park itself in the Piazza Erbe, singing, shouting, guffawing and having a thoroughly good time, directly under my window, until five in the morning. I didn't close my eyes all night.

This night of torture greatly assisted my snobbish bourgeois impulses in their urge to torment me. "This could only have happened to you, you little school-teacher—taking a room like that!" they smirked. "A proper chap would have run a mile. Your father would never have set foot in such a place, and neither would any of your countless relatives. With a floor-level window!"

I was indeed ashamed of myself. Intensely ashamed. All night long.

The following day I got straight on the train and went to Lake Garda. The boat was so crammed that the regular passengers were pushing and shoving each other with their suitcases on the gangway. But I had purchased a first-class ticket and made my way down to the main seating area. I had no view, but I was able to loll around in comfort and was almost alone. I disembarked at Gardone and installed myself in a really good hotel (I mustn't boast—it was also quite cheap: Gardone is the hottest place in northern Italy and there are no high-season rates at that time of year). I took pleasure in the hot water tap, which actually produced wonderfully hot water; in the lunch, where, at long last, the two staple cheeses of Italy, Gorgonzola and Bel Paese, the blonde and brunette varieties, made their appearance; and in the young middle-class clientele—the sort of people you might see in the Forum cinema back in Pest. I grandly exchanged a 500-lira note, and the waiter counted out the great centuries of Italian history onto the table: *trecento… quattrocento… cinquecento*. Then I devoted myself to washing off the last grimy, painful consciousness of proletarianization and placelessness in the cool, dark waters of Lake Garda.

So there you have it: I'm no better than anyone else.

And yet I loathe nothing in the world more than the sense of bourgeois superiority. The bourgeoisie stands in the same relation to the genuine aristocracy as a mosquito priding itself on its class superiority over a flea. I loathe the bourgeois notion of "being of a good family"—which simply means that Pater is now well-to-do because he bought a licensed brothel in Mohács. I loathe bourgeois "civilization", which amounts to little more than "when I die I want hot and cold running water in my tomb". I hate the bourgeois notion of "culture" that underpins the novels of Zsolt Harsányi and Stefan Zweig. I loathe all distinctions based on money, and pseudo-money, and the appearance of money. Money itself I love, and I wouldn't mind having a lot more of it—but not because that would make me a gentleman. I am quite certain that I never will be a gentleman: for that one would need not only a great deal more money and free time than I have, but also a lot more breeding. I might of course pass as a gentleman in the Budapest sense of the word, meaning that I wear a collar and tie, though not always, and that at the very first opportunity I too turn my nose up, just like the rest of my fellow

countrymen. And of course I too believe that my social rank is a matter of finding the right hotel room, eating in the right restaurant and having a suitable seat on the train. But I also know perfectly well that it depends on nothing of a material nature, and that my essential commonness, my innate lower-classness, mean no more than that, in the typical Budapest way, I feel the force of the rules but not the obligations they imply. Such is the power over me of my "good", and therefore thoroughly bad, upbringing.

Fie on you! You should be ashamed of yourself!

Later, I realized that my analysis had been incomplete, and that my malaise had other causes than simply my entrenched snobbery.

HEAT

P EOPLE ARE in general most deeply surprised by two things: one is when something turns out to be completely different from what they have been led to expect, the other when they find it exactly as it had been described. The latter occurs to me much more often.

And so it was with the heat. Everyone had said that the summer in Italy would be very, very hot. At first I thought of it as simply my usual bad luck. Only with time did I begin to realize that it was the natural order of things, something the natives take for granted. The heat starts at four in the morning and lasts until eight at night. There are few hours in between when the temperatures are bearable, and the pattern is not an agreeable one.

I feel hot not only when I go walking. Sometimes I can be sitting and suddenly the heat will envelop me—calmly, serenely, overpoweringly. It feels as if I am stewing in my own juices. Not pleasant.

VITTORIALE

H ERE, in the Vittoriale Palace beside Lake Garda, resides one of the national treasures, D'Annunzio. I looked the place over. Poor old D'Annunzio! Can the tastes of his period really be so passé? Or are the young of Italy right in their savagely ironic view of him as a raw, impotent peasant, and—in their fastidiousness and "good taste"—to see his art as the snobbish affectation of a parvenu, as the English did with Oscar Wilde's decadence?

HOUSE AND
CYPRESS TREE

I TAKE A STROLL between the lakeside mountains, and am gazing around, almost half-consciously, when, with an almost painful sense of wonder, it suddenly strikes me: *this is Italy!* Before me stands a house; in front of it, a cypress tree. Any drawing, of an Egyptian sphinx or pyramid, to give the most obvious example, says more than any photograph can. The pencil simplifies a landscape, condensing it down to its essence, to a motif. The scene before me now represents Italian stylization in its ultimate simplicity: a rectangular, flat-roofed house beside a cypress tree somewhat taller than itself. House and cypress tree: in our Northern winters, beyond the ice wall of the Alps, it will be enough to conjure up this image to myself to feel the whole of Italy coming alive inside me once again.

"The cypress standing guard in front of the house": a literary cliché. But, like most clichés, profoundly true. The cypress really does seem to stand guard:

solemn to the point of pomposity and at the same time inspiring in its nobility and fidelity—like the faithful St Bernard dog.

SOLITUDE

A MONG THE TRULY LONELY I class those who are alone very seldom, and then perhaps only in moments set aside for reading or writing. My profession, schoolteaching, by its very nature forces even the most highly strung person into contact with others; and then, in the evening, a certain anxiety verging on panic drives him back into company.

I have been alone here for several days now. Apart from seeking information and making arrangements, I have exchanged not a word with anyone. It is the first time in my life that I have been on my own for so long.

It quite astonishes me how little I miss human company. I would never have thought how well I would get by without conversation and companionship. For advice I go to Baedeker. He serves as my real friend. He thinks of everything, tells me where I should go. Anything I really want to say is committed to a notepad.

I can feel the good this solitude is doing me. My thoughts arrange themselves in longer sequences. My feelings are more intense, and I see their outlines more clearly. Chaotic thoughts are reduced to order, and almost everything welling up inside me spills out and ripens toward form and expression.

It is a comfort to know that I have discovered this panacea, even if it won't always be part of my life.

THE PEOPLE'S TRAIN

T HE JOURNEY from Gardone to Bologna takes almost a full day. The section by boat is delightful, but the train from Desenzano to Bologna proves rather less so. It stops for five to ten minutes at every station, the passengers get off, and then get back on. It is called, with the gentle irony of the Italians, the *accelerato.*

It is incredible how deep-rooted the urge to travel lies in the national character. Every so often the whole family will jump up and set off with their *bambini* and huge boxes of luggage to visit the other end of the boot. According to the newspapers, this year, on the 15th and 16th of August (a Saturday and Sunday), some 750,000 people over and above the usual traffic (itself always considerable) were on the move across the country. On the cheapest trains alone, the *treni popolari*, there were possibly 150,000. But in fact every train here is a low-fare people's train. No one travels at the full rate. Everyone has some document or other qualifying them for a huge concessionary discount.

As I gaze around at the travel-subsidized hordes I am struck by how cheerful, how proud and friendly they are—how quickly they get to know each other and how much they have to say. Yes, these are the proud sons and daughters of the totalitarian state, of Fascism triumphant. This is the Italian people. Here everything happens in their name: at their bidding run the cut-price trains; for their sake new buildings—the new Italian cities—are thrown up; for their delectation strut the endless military parades; for love of them, Abyssinia was conquered.

The people's trains run back and forth across a state owned by the people. I'm no master of the details, but it is said, and I see it in their faces, that things are better here for the masses than they are anywhere else—a thousand times better than at home in Hungary—in terms of material satisfaction, and given the modest demands of the population… But, on a moral or ethical level, this immeasurably inflated patriotic self-esteem has transformed every Italian into a hero, puffed him up into a citizen of a second Roman Imperium.

Sitting here on the train I have the feeling that, compared to anywhere else, the people are altogether more of a body: the social strata are less sharply divided from one another, their boundaries dissolved in the shared

Fascist enthusiasm. They are a "people" not only in the socialist sense of the word: they are first and foremost the *Italian* people.

Yes, it's all very wonderful, and wonderful the countless social achievements of Fascism. I can't tell you right now exactly how many thousands of unemployed have been given work in the sugar mills, or how many thousands of those in work (sometimes an entire trade, on a corporate basis) have had their wages increased (how can an industrialist do otherwise than bow to the wishes of the state?)—but... How can I put this?...

Every day I read a local paper. It's rather like the one written specially for the elder Rockefeller in which only agreeable and reassuring news is reported. Everywhere in the world, and especially in Spain, the Italian spirit is triumphant. Here in Italy, only magnificent things occur. Il Duce opens a new tortoise-racing stadium, and the people rejoice. The heir to the throne makes an appearance in the uniform of a high-ranking officer in the Sea Scouts movement, and the people rejoice. The Duke of Aosta blows the Day of Atonement trumpet for the Jewish community in Milan, and the people rejoice. The Italian people live in a perpetual state of rejoicing. Everything here is just fine. God on high smiles down on his people.

Yes, I know that the Italians are a childlike people, but that still doesn't help me understand how they can bear it—this non-stop, unceasing celebration, this relentless mass euphoria. It's as terrifying as the Day of Salvation.

Lucifer has been totally expelled from the Italian heaven. Nothing unpleasant or malicious is reported in the newspapers. They appear to be written not by journalists but by celestial angels. Everyone is thoroughly contented. When you get into conversation with people on the train, you hear only the same stereotypical phrases that you read in the papers. They are as perfectly conditioned as Huxley's humanity of the future. The moment you volunteer anything to the contrary, they fall silent and become deadly serious. But wasn't this once the home of Arnaldo da Brescia, of Cola di Rienzi, of Silvio Pellico, of Garibaldi and the Carbonari, those archetypal discontents and rebels?

And yes, even I would agree that there is nothing more important in life than to help folk in their misery, to raise the fallen, to contribute materially and morally to the lives of ordinary people. Especially to the poor of the Earth (a phrase that here too is used in jest). So long as people continue to live in slavery any talk of the New Breed of Men is no more than a fine phrase in the mouth of a tycoon—laughable humbug. But is it not enough, then, to live as man was meant to? Or is it also necessary to be "happy"? Who is happy? The madman, the drunk, the subject of hypnosis or of auto-suggestion. Man in his natural state is dissatisfied. Anyone who is not should be treated with suspicion. So… are the Italians paying too high a price for their escape from chaos and oppression?

I recently read the book by the émigré Count Sforza, in which he shows that the great creative periods in Italy have always been those when it was divided into little city states, forever blighted by misfortune and tearing each other to pieces; whereas the dream of a great empire has always coincided with times of spiritual and intellectual barrenness.

One of the slogans and celebratory patriotic phrases I regularly see inscribed on the walls of houses here is the declaration: *Meglio vivere un giorno da leone che cent'anni da pecora*—Better to live one day as a lion than a hundred years as a lamb. But I have to wonder: if Dante were to rise from the dead and revisit the city of his birth and the landscapes of Tuscany and Ravenna, would he not see that same sentence emblazoned on the forehead of today's Italy?

Italy, the scene of Dante's solitudes, the home of Cellini's madmen, once the domain of individual pride, has become a country of the self-satisfaction of the masses. Fascism has all the appearance of a great dictatorship based on the cult of a single personality, but the truth is that embodied in the personality cult and working through it is a dictatorship of the people—the unified and eternally happy people. This is the greatest political paradox of our time: that whereas in nominally democratic Britain real power lies in the hands of the elite, in the dictatorships it is held by the masses.

BOLOGNA

NOT MUCH is written or said about this city. Most visitors turn up here more or less by chance and are astonished by the charm and vitality of the place. Many of the streets are lined with arcades, beneath which you find wonderful shop windows, throngs of sophisticated people and superb coffee houses, and there are imposing historical monuments. The medieval home (and former prison) of Prince Enzo stands ringed by Gothic and Renaissance palazzi. Beside it is a statue of Neptune, one of Italy's most envy-inspiring spectacles, since cold water flows steadily down its four sides. The great cities dating from this period—Bologna, Venice, Florence—are all of an ideal size. They have a quarter of a million inhabitants, but are spared the narrow streets and confined public spaces of smaller towns. They are all genuine cities, without the usual hordes of recent arrivals and run-down central areas. They are human-scale. One of the greatest shortcomings of Hungarian civilization is that we have no cities of this type and size.

On my first evening there I simply followed my nose and discovered a charming little *trattoria*, where they prepared a wonderful *fritto misto* for me, after which I drank a few glasses of a very agreeable *Albano dolce*. I always enjoy eating and drinking, but now that I am alone it is my chief pleasure and source of stimulation. This comes with solitude, it seems. I now understand the hearty appetite of Edvardas Turauskas, as well as his horror of loneliness.

Like him, I am eating and drinking a shocking amount. I want to savour every dish and every variety of beverage that Italy has to offer. My greatest regret is that in this heat I don't always have much desire for wine. Sometimes in the evenings I set out to taste some really good local vintages and end up drinking orange juice. But I am not a real gourmet. I don't have much feeling for the subtler nuances of Italian food and wine. It doesn't matter to me how good they are, but how new to me, how unfamiliar. I am an incurable romantic.

I had finished the agreeable *Albano dolce* and was on my way back to the hotel when I had one of the most astonishing experiences of my entire trip. I was strolling contentedly along in the gloom when suddenly, as I entered one of the squares, a vision rose up before me— two enormous leaning towers, inclined at such an angle

I thought I must be drunk. One soared up on my right, the other on the left, wobbling about in the silence and darkness and filling me with terror. They were Asinelli and Garisenda. They were as grotesquely fearsome and medieval in style as some of the poems of Milán Füst.

Later I learnt from Baedeker that these towers are the most famous landmark in Bologna. I am afraid even I should have known about them. I fear I am rather like the notorious American lady, Mrs Green, who tells us in the recently published account of her Italian travels that "the Tiber is a truly magnificent river, despite the fact that no one has ever heard of it".

But to get back to the towers. Along with the serenity of Italy there is also a horrific side: the silent cypresses beside the cemeteries, the pitch-black alleyways, the rooftops bristling with battlements, the slanting towers. They correspond to something in the Italian soul. In his letters Shelley writes about the natives as if they were terrifying semi-savages, and to this day something of that lingers on in them. It is no accident that in their moments of grandeur they like to put on black shirts and go marauding, or march around in procession dressed up as bandits.

RAVENNA

THE ACTUAL CITY is small and oppressive. The mayor leaves no stone unturned to ensure that the inhabitants are comfortable, and as a result the town is scattered with stone inscriptions advising you that, due to the narrowness of the street ahead, it is impossible to proceed, except by jumping from stone to stone, on one leg. The place feels abandoned, grim, deathlike. And no wonder. Ravenna has known three golden ages, the third ending in the eighth century AD, and it has decayed steadily ever since. No other city in Europe has been in a state of decay for so long. There is a particular reason for this: neither moral collapse nor politics, but geography. Ravenna was once a city on a lagoon, and before the rise of Venice it played the same role that its luckier rival did later, trading between the two shores of the Adriatic, and it was here, at nearby Classe, that the ancient naval harbour was built. But then the sea abandoned Ravenna. The lagoon dried up and filled with sand, and the city was left high and dry, like a stranded fish.

It continues to decay. The heat, the dust and the mosquitoes are made even more oppressive by the toxic fumes of a fertilizer factory, the presence of which can be felt in every part of the town. Whatever would the d'Estes and the Polentas have thought of this stench of industry?

But why do I always invoke these local petty tyrants, and why do they haunt my journey? Because one or two of them are of genuine interest, if not very much, and because they created buildings and a handful of imposing tombs to glorify their names beyond the grave. And because, every now and then—Cangrande in Verona and Guido Novello in Ravenna—they opened their houses to Dante.

Well, then: because they opened their houses to Dante, and because it was in this same abandoned Ravenna that Dante died and was buried, under the protection of Guido Novello. A gesture of which none of today's petty tyrants would be capable.

So, this was the real goal of my travels, this run-down and evil-smelling town. It was one of the most passionate dreams of my youth to stand in person before the famous Byzantine mosaics, so faithfully preserved in the ancient basilica in Ravenna.

BYZANTIUM

T HE MOSAICS THEMSELVES—and this was the most surprising thing—did not disappoint. The moment I first caught sight of one I was seized by an intense perturbation. But perhaps that emotion really referred back to my youth, to a period from which all that remained was this urge to see Ravenna.

About these mosaics, the basilica itself and the fifteen-hundred-year-old burial sites, I have little to say that isn't a commonplace of art history. The greatest surprise was simply that they are what they are. As art they were certainly no disappointment. What I had been told was all perfectly true: especially what I had always believed, that the Byzantine background in which the mosaics are placed is all of a uniform colour—a kind of gold, or a harrowing dark blue, or a wonderfully warm golden green. Below it is another field, bearing scenes of nature, hills and trees. But no one had mentioned how very different, how unexpectedly warm, is the interior of a basilica in which the windows are made of alabaster. The faces of the Emperor Justinian's retinue

ICTORIM·SCA·PAVLINA·SCA·EMERENTIANA·SCA·DARIA·SCA·ANASTASIA·SCA·IVSTINA·SC

are surprisingly modern, but that I already knew from reproductions.

What moves one is the sheer antiquity. One begins to look on the Gothic intrusions and restorations with increasing resentment. How very parvenu, one thinks: mere thirteenth century! In these Byzantine images you find an almost baffling unity: on the one hand, a kind of urbane world-weariness, a courtly effeminacy in the gestures and faces; and on the other, a primitive innocence of technique. This two-sidedness is best seen in the heads of the columns in Sant'Apollinare Nuovo. Each has a double capital, an elaborately worked (and rather fine) Corinthian one, with a second immediately over it, the real one, that supports the arch above—a simple, unworked mass of stone, narrowing as it rises and covered in Byzantine religious symbols.

THE TOMB OF
DIETRICH VON BERN

YOU PICK YOUR WAY across the railway tracks, registering the fumes of the fertilizer factory with redoubled strength, continue along a dusty main road for ten minutes, and there stands the tomb of Theodoric the Great. It is the strangest mausoleum I have yet seen in Italy. It is like nothing else: somehow not quite European. It is a message from the teeming, labyrinthine gloom of the first thousand years of Christianity, which Spengler describes as the "Arabian" or "Magical" period. The top consists of a formidable monolith. The interior is bare, with a huge porphyry bathtub in it—I have no idea why—and below it the grave. Here lies the ruler of the Ostrogoths. Here reposes the greatest dream of the Germanic peoples.

For it was here that the two leading powers of Europe, German and Byzantine, met in conflict. My present journey almost exactly follows the route of their struggle. The wild hunter Dietrich von Bern first appears in

Verona; near Ravenna he fought a great battle—the *Rabenschlacht* of the thousand-year-old German sagas. Ravenna was the seat of the Byzantine generals, the heroic Belisarius and the eunuch Narses, and here the Goths, with their strength fading, attacked under Vitigis and Totila. The last Gothic king, Tejas, was killed with his valiant army further down the peninsula, on the slopes of Vesuvius. Almost all traces of the heretical Goths have now vanished. They were Arians, and there is still a street in Ravenna named after them. One of the better-known tombs was once an Arian baptistery. And here stands the mausoleum of Dietrich von Bern, a relic of one of the greatest battles in human history.

And it goes on still... Even as I stood above the grave of Dietrich von Bern, Spanish government troops were being slaughtered in the Guadarrama pass and the insurgents were firing their last rounds at the Toledo Alcázar. But the war in Spain has long ceased to be a struggle between rebels and government forces. It has become a clash of two opposing worlds: two versions of collectivism finally joined in open conflict. Now the other nations of Europe stand poised around the Spanish ring, armed to the teeth and holding on to one another's hands, lest they rush to the aid of one of the combatants—before counting up to nine over whichever goes down, and hurling themselves at one another to establish, through warfare, whichever of the two had been right. Byzantium and the Goths, East and West, Orthodox and Arian (Arians/Aryans: the names echo, as if history were making a pun). Once the battle was for Rome. Now it is for the whole of Europe.

But on that occasion, in the last analysis neither side really won. That was a third power: the Byzantines destroyed the Eastern Goths, only for their Gothic cousins, the Lombards, to drive them out in turn—and then promptly vanish, almost without trace, after giving their name to one of the great regions of Italy. And Rome became neither Arian nor Greek Orthodox, but Roman and Catholic. Perhaps today too there is still hope (pray for this, venerable St Athanasius and all you anti-heretical Early Church Fathers!) that once again a third power should come victoriously between the two.

SAN MARINO

I WENT ON TO RIMINI, that endlessly elongated Italian version of our own Siófok, where I bathed in the Adriatic after lunch, then took a seat on the little electric train up to San Marino. I had thought that I would be the only person mad enough to set out on such an outing immediately after lunch, in such appalling heat. But I was wrong. The little train was no less crammed than any of the others I had been on. Whole hordes were on their way to San Marino. It seems I am by no means the only madman here. Tripping up to San Marino in these temperatures is apparently quite the norm. What shall we do next? I know—after lunch, let's all go up to San Marino.

San Marino is a mountaintop town, the most extreme example of those I have seen so far. It is much more mountainous than Gubbio, cowering on the side of its bleak prominence, or the terrifyingly black, Papal-medieval Anagni, or Orvieto, laid out like a huge board game on a table. It rises both higher and more abruptly than any of these. The cliff on which it is built is absolutely vertical on one side, as if cut by a knife; the other is terrain for rock-climbers. One cannot begin to fathom what was in the minds of the people who colonized and built it. It really is a place where, if you lose your footing, you plummet headlong out of the town.

The route becomes increasingly romantic as it rises. From the broad plains of Romagna you get your first, distant views of the quaint mountain republic, with its three crests, the three towers built on its peak. The train climbs steadily towards it, burrowing through tunnels and weaving its way back and forth like the miniature cave railway in Városliget, emerging suddenly on one side, then on the other, ever higher and higher, while the miraculous little town comes steadily into view, with the three towers above it.

Finally we reach the top. But even now there is still nothing above us for quite a way. The little train empties the tourists out and they climb cheerfully upwards, vying eagerly with each other. They pass through the town gate and set off up the steep streets of the tiny centre. They reach the miniature piazza, where the diminutive city hall stands, every bit as ancient and wonderful as the *palazzi comunali* of many far grander cities. Little restaurants on every side invite one to try their views, their music and their *moscato* wine (the local speciality).

People are already seated and gazing in admiration at the republican army, of which at least half the entire personnel must be strolling up and down in front of the town hall. Others simply race up to the post office, then stream back down to the waiting train, clutching postcards covered in San Marino stamps.

But the enthusiastic majority continue bravely along the cliff road towards the towers. It leads directly up the mountain, with chasms plunging away to left and right. The towers are genuinely medieval, although much restored—fortified bastions ruling fantastically over the landscape below, like the old tyrant rulers of the clans, every one of them a Malatesta, a Scaliger, or a Rovere, though the eagle-feather emblem at the top of each, the symbol of San Marino, tames them, as you would a bird. The tourists swarm happily up and down the steps (which have no guard rails), no doubt naively rejoicing in the fact that they "didn't have to live in those olden times"—rather like the first-time spectators at a boxing match who congratulate themselves on not being the ones getting knocked about.

THE THIRD TOWER

T HUS WE ARRIVED at a little gate bearing the notice: Road to the Third Tower. Having carried them this far, the day-trippers' enthusiasm instantly deserted them. Puffing and panting, they turned back and made for the viewpoints and the *moscato*. I continued on— suddenly, happily, at ease and alone. The third tower was all mine.

The tower stands apart, at the far corner of the mountain top, on an inaccessible cliff, very steep on both sides. The town itself doesn't extend this far, and as you pick your way to the end of the crest you are made giddy by the height. Here, on the exposed ridge, a chill wind blows, even in this intense heat. I imagine it must do so at all times.

I sit at the foot of the tower and gaze out at the view. My view. So far I have been obliged to share it with the day-trippers, to join enthusiastically in their constant chattering. Now I have come into possession of my soul. The whole of this part of the country is mine: on one side, rich, twilit Romagna, with its scattering of towns, sloping gently down to the distant sea; and on the other, the bandit-haunted Apennines of ancient Etruria. Behind them again, I sense the presence of my Easter kingdom: Urbino, Arezzo, Gubbio, and the whole of Umbria. These are real mountains, as vast as a man could wish. Mountains any larger than these I do not like. I dislike the Alps. They are excessive, unmanageable, titanic. In a word, inhuman. No mountain should be greater than these before me. The Apennines are human-scale, just as the whole Italian landscape is human-scale. And that is why it is lovelier than any other.

I sit looking out over the Italian countryside. In the advancing twilight the blues and the reds on the skyline have a serenity of inexpressible sweetness, and for the first time on my present journey I am happy. Happy in the archaic sense of the word, according to which no child can be said to be happy: a replete happiness, containing everything. The Third Tower is mine alone. Italy is mine, not Mussolini's. I am mine alone: alone in my self-completeness.

There, at the foot of the Third Tower, I understood everything. My restlessness—on the train, in the various hotels and inns, in the periods between excursions, indeed whenever during the entire journey I had been forced into contact with that collectivity of the lonely,

the euphoric Italian collectivity. I shielded my solitari-
ness from them, and from the European future that
they represented for me. I felt my solitary happiness
threatened by their happiness of the herd, because they
were stronger than I was.

The happiness I feel here at the foot of the Third
Tower is something I must not give up for anyone: for
anyone, or anything. I cannot surrender my soul to any
nation state, or to any set of beliefs.

FERRARA

I**N TIME** you get used to it. Having been on the road for two to three weeks, I now find it quite natural. You arrive in a town towards evening. You ask your way to the square, throw a glance over the palazzo, with its vast tower and bristling battlements, and seek out the inevitable, everywhere-the-same *albergo* that comes with it. You dine, drink a little wine, and the next morning you tour the town. There is always a cathedral, a slanting tower, and some unique local attraction. In Ferrara, for example, it is the d'Este Castle: ancient, forbidding and grim, in the very heart of the town and surrounded by a moat filled with water. Later, in the evening, this moat came to inspire a certain respect, though I had my suspicions of it from the first. Sadly, my worst fears were to be realized.

In the hotel, when I went to draw back the curtain and open the window, the chambermaid stopped me and pointed out the great number of *zanzare*: mosquitoes. She was right. My suspicions of that moat had been fully justified. None of these great medieval institutions comes without some drawback. I barely closed my eyes the entire night. Since then I have always thought bad thoughts about the d'Estes. And yet, if the Scaligers and the Polentas opened their doors to Dante, they did the same for Ariosto and Tasso. The latter, it's true, went mad in their care.

Baedeker had mentioned the danger with reference to Ravenna: *Im Sommer viele Stechmücken*. Now why should the German word be so much more comical than its Hungarian or Italian equivalents? What is so utterly impossible about a *Stechmücke*, compared to a *nünüke* or a *rézsüke*?

The *Stechmücken* were, for me, analogous with the heat. I had heard so much about them that I had ceased to believe it, and the first time I awoke with an inflamed and puffy head (in Verona) I felt deeply offended. They have been the faithful companions of my journey ever since. They are much more nimble than the mosquitoes of our own Margaret Island.

TRIESTE, OR, IN A WORD, EXHAUSTION

T RIESTE IS a really fine city, by nature of its quarter of a million contending ideals. I take a look at a cathedral, then a castle, then the sea.

Along the Corso Emmanuel, one of the principal streets, I notice a shop window full of enamel chamber pots. Below them is the proclamation: "Our national enamelware competes with the best in the world!" Well, so it does. But all the same, these Italians… They are certainly not to be trifled with. They will vie with anyone, and, when they choose to, they certainly let you know. Everything here is done for the greater glory of the nation.

Trieste feels somehow like home. It is a product, like myself, of the Dual Monarchy. Its streets are wide—impressive Austro-Hungarian streets. The buildings are aligned in symmetrical patterns, like the side whiskers of Franz Joseph. The beer is cold and wonderful, just as it is at home. After all that wine and orange juice, I can't get enough of it. The women are blonde and beautiful. Apropos of which… it will indeed be good to go home.

Yes, the time has come. I am tired. And perhaps I don't love Italy all that much. Just as, it seems, I don't love anyone or anything "all that much". Even myself I can no longer love as tenderly and attentively as when I was younger.

I am tired. It will be very good to go home. The panic is over, I have calmed down, my inner reserves are exhausted. Somehow, all it needs now is courage. Just don't surrender your solitude for anything or anyone. How does Milton's Satan put it? "What matter where, if I be still the same?" Whatever becomes of Europe, trust in your inner stars. Somewhere, always, a Third Tower will be waiting for you.

It's enough.

LIST OF
ILLUSTRATIONS

p. 32 · Piazza San Marco, Venice
© *2013 Getty Images*

p. 47 · Exterior view of the Villa Rotonda Palladiana in Vicenza
© *Bettmann / CORBIS*

p. 56 · Piazza delle Erbe in Verona with the market, 1936
© *Mary Evans / Alinari Archives*

p. 60 · Beach promenade of Gardone Riviera on Lake Garda, 1935
© *Mary Evans / SZ Photo / Scherl*

p. 72 · Façade of the central station of Milan, *c.* 1935
© *Mary Evans / Alinari Archives*

p. 81 · The two towers, Bologna
© *Mary Evans Picture Library / Pump Park Photography*

p. 86 · The theory of the Virgins and Saints, detail of the mosaic
decoration, in the Church of Sant'Apollinare Nuovo, Ravenna
© *Alinari Archives, Florence / Mary Evans*

p. 90 · The Mausoleum of Theodoric, Ravenna
© *Alinari via Getty Images*

p. 105 · Miramare Castle, Trieste
© *Walter Sanders*

Pushkin Press

Pushkin Press was founded in 1997, and publishes novels, essays, memoirs, children's books—everything from timeless classics to the urgent and contemporary.

This book is part of the Pushkin Collection of paperbacks, designed to be as satisfying as possible to hold and to enjoy. It is typeset in Monotype Baskerville, based on the transitional English serif typeface designed in the mid-eighteenth century by John Baskerville. It was litho-printed on Munken Premium White Paper and notch-bound by the independently owned printer TJ International in Padstow, Cornwall. The cover, with French flaps, was printed on Colorplan Pristine White paper. The paper and cover board are both acid-free and Forest Stewardship Council (FSC) certified.

Pushkin Press publishes the best writing from around the world—great stories, beautifully produced, to be read and read again.